UNMUTED

My Journey to Overcoming Silence and Finding Freedom

RECIA KABBAH

UNMUTED

I have tried to recreate events, locales and conversations from my memories of them. In order to maintain their anonymity in some instances, I have changed the names of individuals and places. I may have changed some identifying characteristics and details such as physical properties, occupations and places of residence.

For permission requests, write to the publisher, addressed:

Jacinth Media Productions
52 N. 2nd Street
Coplay, PA 18037

All Scripture quotes are taken from the Holy Bible, King James Version, Cambridge, 1769; and The ESV® Bible
(The Holy Bible, English Standard Version®).
ESV® Text Edition: 2016. Copyright © 2001 by Crossway,
A publishing ministry of Good News Publishers.

Library of Congress Control Number: 2023912039
Paperback-ISBN: 978-1-960594-06-8
Hardback-ISBN: 978-1-960594-19-8
Ebook-ISBN: 978-1-960594-07-5
This book was printed in the United States
First Printing
10 9 8 7 6 5 4 3 2 1
Book cover design by Jacinth Media Productions

Dear God,

As I welcome my readers to embark on this journey with me, I ask for your guidance and blessings. Please help them find peace and solace within the pages of this book and give them insight and understanding from my pain. May they be uplifted by the hope and resilience that I have found in the face of adversity, and may they find inspiration to overcome their own challenges. Please grant me strength and courage as I share my story with honesty, vulnerability and offer comfort and encouragement to those who are struggling. God, thank you for this opportunity to share my experiences and to connect with others through my writing. I pray that my words bring healing and transformation to all who read them. Amen.

"In thee, O LORD, do I put my trust; let me never be ashamed: deliver me in thy righteousness." Psalm 31:1 KJV

Table of Content

Dedication

To all those who have ever felt silenced by their pain and trauma, this book is dedicated to you. It is a testimony to the fact that no matter how deep your wounds may be, there is always hope for healing and growth. To my loved ones who have stood by me through the darkest of times, thank you for your unwavering support and belief in me. To my three beautiful children who gave me a stronger purpose in motherhood. I would not be here today to write this book if it weren't for you.

To my late grandaunt who just passed away during the time I was writing this book: you gave me a higher purpose to push through my trauma and grief to complete this book. You are the reason why I migrated from Liberia to the United States. You are responsible for my new beginning, and I hope that I made you proud. Words alone can't express my gratitude for you. Rest in power and peace. To the people who have inspired me to keep going and constantly reminded me that I am not alone in my struggles, I can't thank you enough.

Finally, to all the young girls back home in Liberia who feel trapped and silenced by their pain and lack of opportunities. You are more powerful than you think. The power lies deep within you. Don't wait for anyone to hand you an opportunity when you can create it for yourself with the gifts that lie within you. I want you all to find the strength and courage to break free from the chains of silence and reclaim your voice. May this book serve as a reminder of the power that lies within us all.

Introduction

Muted by Pain

Have you ever felt muted? Felt stuck and silenced by your pain? That was me. So many of us are walking around muted by hurt, betrayal, resentment, neglect, hate, abuse, and filled with so much anger stacked on top of unhealed pain. We struggle with the weight of keeping our family's secrets safe despite how much it hurts and how detrimental it is to our personal growth. Being "muted" by your pain makes it hard to express yourself fully. Feeling silenced by the weight of emotional pain is crushing.

When we're in the midst of deep emotional pain, it can feel like we're trapped behind an invisible wall. We can see the people around us, but we can't connect with them in the way that we want to. We block the possibility of creating relationships out of fear and not being able to trust others. We feel silenced and stuck as if our words are stuck in our throats, and we feel like we're screaming but no one is listening. We've been muted by our pain. The pain can be so intense that it takes over our entire being, making it difficult to do anything. The pain is all we can think about, but we can't find the words to express it. It's like being trapped in a cage with no way out. We want to break free and share our pain with others, but we don't know how and we're afraid.

Feeling muted by my pain was an isolating and overwhelming experience. I felt trapped in a dark and silent world, where expressing my emotions became an uphill battle. It was important for me to remember that struggling to find my voice was completely normal, and seeking support was a crucial step in finding my way back to the surface. By acknowledging and processing my pain, I was able to begin dismantling the barriers that kept me muted and took small steps towards healing and breaking the silence. Join me on this journey as I share how I transformed from being muted to becoming unsilenced. Together, we will discover the power of reclaiming our voices and embracing the healing process.

CHAPTER 1
A Motherless Child

My story begins in a small town called Lazelemai, in Liberia, West Africa. As a young African woman, life was simple yet filled with love. I was the youngest of four children and cherished by my mother, father, and older siblings.

One day, everything changed. I woke up to my parents packing our belongings, but they never explained why they packed us up. At five years old, my father took my sister and me to visit our aunt in a different city and he never returned. This short visit felt like a lifetime. Time stood still and I longed for the warm embrace of my mother, father, and other siblings left behind.

I always knew I shared a special bond with my mother. I cried out countless nights, screaming her name, but she never showed up. I quickly learned the true definition of a motherless child. I longed for my mother's touch and from that day on. No one held me like my mother held me. Two years passed, and I discovered that my mother had fallen seriously ill and passed away. I remember the elders coming to take us back home for her funeral. Everyone was crying and I joined them, though I didn't fully understand the magnitude of losing a loved one, especially my mother. I never got to say goodbye properly or see her one last time. The pain of being a motherless child became my constant companion. I never got to see my mother's body. I never got that closure I needed as a child. I guess my elders were trying to protect me from grieving the loss of my mother.

Following my mother's wishes, my family sent me to live with her best friend in the capital city, Monrovia. While my mother was pregnant with me, she had gotten terminally ill. Her best friend was there for her through it all. My mother's dying wish was for her best friend to raise me as her daughter if anything happened to her. It was a difficult transition. Not only had I lost my mother, but I was also far from my father and siblings in our village. I felt lost and out of place yearning for my mother's touch and crying out for her presence. As I grew older, family members started to tell me stories about my past in hopes of gaining a better under-standing of what my mother was like as a friend, as a woman

Living with my new mom from the age of eight to sixteen, was a different experience. As my mom's best friend, she did her best to fill the void left by my mother, but it was never the same. I craved the love, nurturing, and emotional connection only a mother could provide. Seeking love in the wrong places became my refuge and the streets became my temporary home. Hanging out in the streets became my comfort zone. I hoped to feel a sense of belonging and love. I remember crying daily and screaming out my mother's name and longing for her embrace. I used to wish to dream of my mother because I had no memories of her. So, I prayed for God to reveal my mother to me in my dreams so that I could remember those images of her. I just wanted her to appear at least once in my dreams since I would never see her in person ever again.

Living with my new mom was not always a fairytale, but she did her best to take care of me and I will forever be grateful to her. Although my new mom cared for me, our relationship changed when she remarried. I doubt that she had any idea how this affected our relationship and created distance between us. Her new husband was controlling, and I felt like a stranger in my own home. I once again felt silenced because I felt out of place, became invisible, and I was falsely accused and punished for things I didn't do. No one stood up for me and I felt powerless. As a child, I struggled to understand the complexities of life, unable to rely solely on my guardians for protection.

Around the age of sixteen, my new mom decided she had enough of me roaming around the streets and dealing with boys. She was concerned that I may get pregnant, and she didn't want to be the blame. She sent me to live with my uncle, my mother's younger brother. She believed that a fresh start with structure and discipline would be best for me. My uncle was a well-respected man in his community. A well-respected soldier in the army of Liberia, became my new guardian, offering safety and a chance for a better future.

I will forever be grateful for the love and care my second mommy has shown me over the years. As my mother's best friend, she kept her promise and I truly believe my mother would have been pleased. Mom, thank you for your unconditional love, guidance, and for fulfilling the promises you made to my mom. I am so grateful to have you in my life, and I love you dearly.

CHAPTER 2

Feeling Alone

Here we go again. Just as I was starting to feel at home, I found myself packing up and moving to a new city, leaving behind my friends, and adopted siblings. The constant cycle of bouncing from one home to another is indescribable. After finally settling in with my new family, I was forced to start over once more. During this new transition, I felt numb, as if I didn't belong all over again. It was like reliving the nightmare of being a motherless child. The constant shuffling from home to home made my young heart feel unworthy, unloved, and unwanted.

My mom thought she was doing what was best for me by sending me to live with my uncle, but it backfired. My uncle was supposed to be my protector, guiding, and leading me. However, he became the source of my deepest pain. I vividly remember being silenced by his abuse. At

seventeen, I felt an overwhelming sense of worthlessness due to the physical abuse of which he subjected me. It feels strange even speaking about it, let alone writing it down. But I refuse
to remain silent any longer.

Growing up, I never had a father figure since my own father gave me up when I was five. I had hoped my uncle would fill that void, but instead, he worsened my insecurities and further silenced me. The breaking point came when he raped me. His last words, *"You're out there looking for men. I have what you're looking for."* These words and his actions still haunt me, causing me to cringe whenever they resurface in my mind. He attacked me, attempting to overpower and control me. I screamed for help, but no one was there to rescue me. How could a seventeen-year-old girl defend herself against a larger, stronger man? I fought back, but the weight of that helpless girl, lying there lifeless, numb, and silenced by my own flesh and blood, continues to burden me.

The scars I carry serve as a constant reminder of him and the painful past I endured. After the rape and ongoing abuse, I felt empty, disgusted, and embarrassed. How could the person who was supposed to love and protect me become my abuser? The experience took a severe toll on me, both physically and emotionally.

Living with my uncle was unbearable, but I had nowhere else to go and no other choice. To avoid going home, I began wandering the streets and staying out late. This led me to engage in activities I am deeply ashamed to recall. I would spend time with friends and boys, desperate to avoid returning home. Sneaking in late at night became my routine, hoping that my uncle would not hear me. However, he always knew whenever I arrived home late. He would wait up for me and start beating me every time I came home after midnight. I endured countless beatings, which became my new norm, leaving me numb. The scars on my body from those beatings served as a permanent reminder. Even though I tried not to dwell on the painful memories of my past, I cannot deny their existence. My pain is real and will forever be a part of me. I remind myself that while these scars may never fade, they do not define me or hold me captive to my past.

As a younger version of myself, I wrestled with whom I could confide in or share my secret. Who would even believe me? I never entertained the thought of telling anyone about what had happened to me because I knew I would be ignored and disbelieved. In my culture, such matters are not meant to be discussed openly. Everything is kept as a secret, and one is not permitted to talk openly about anything that may disgrace the family name. Revealing such topics can result in being ostracized, neglected, and labeled as a liar. These family secrets are meant to stay within the confines of our household. They should not be shared with neighbors or brought outside of our homes. For years, I had to hold on to these secrets even when I had the urge to confide in my leaders or mentors. The shame I felt prevented me from opening up, keeping me in a place of darkness and causing immense trauma. Shame also bred resentment in my heart towards him, leading to a lack of trust in anyone, especially men.

GENERATIONAL IMPACT:

Having daughters of my own has heightened my desire to protect them from becoming victims of abuse. This has made me overly cautious and vigilant, always trying to keep my children sheltered. However, this overprotection has at times caused resentment from my kids towards me. They have no idea of the struggles I have endured. I cannot comprehend telling them that my actions came from the things I experienced in my childhood. I hope that by sharing my story now, my children will come to understand and appreciate what I have been through, and why I have become the woman I am today.

We all carry an immense burden of guilt, shame, and disappointment from our past traumas. Our trauma has kept us muted and silenced for far too long. I invite all of you to join me on this movement of being "UNMUTED." By speaking my truth, I am not only freeing myself but also helping to liberate others from the chains of abuse and pain. I am sharing my truth and mentally releasing myself from the scars that bind me. No one can take away my power ever again. Thank God I don't resemble what I have endured.

WAYS TO HEAL FROM SEXUAL ABUSE:

Healing from sexual abuse can be a difficult and complex process, but it is possible with the right support and resources. Here are some steps that may help someone on their healing journey:

1. Seek professional help: A mental health professional can provide emotional support, help you process your experiences, and provide coping strategies. They can also help you address any mental health conditions that may have arisen because of the abuse.

2. Connect with support networks: Talking to someone who has had similar experiences can be incredibly healing. Support groups can provide a safe space for survivors to connect and share their stories.

3. Practice self-care: Taking care of your physical and emotional well-being is important for your healing. This might include activities like exercise, meditation, or spending time with loved ones.

4. Acknowledge and process your feelings: It's important to allow yourself to feel and process the emotions that come up because of the abuse. These emotions can include anger, sadness, guilt, and fear.

5. Reclaim your power: Sexual abuse can rob a person of their sense of power and control. Finding ways to regain a sense of control, through therapy, self-defense classes, or advocacy work can be empowering.

6. Be patient with yourself: Healing from sexual abuse is a journey, not a destination. It's important to be patient with yourself and allow yourself to move through the process at your own pace.

It's important to remember that everyone heals differently and there is no right or wrong way to heal from sexual abuse. It's also important to seek help if you are struggling with thoughts of suicide, self-harm, or other forms of self-harm.

It's common for survivors of sexual abuse to feel isolated and alone. However, there are ways to cope with these feelings and find support. Here are some suggestions:

1. Reach out to loved ones: Surrounding yourself with people who care about you and are supportive can help you feel less alone. People who can be there for you emotionally may include family members, friends, or romantic partners.

2. Join a support group: Support groups for survivors of sexual abuse can provide a sense of community and a safe space to connect with others who have had similar experiences.

3. Talk to a therapist: A mental health professional can provide a supportive and non-judgmental space to process your feelings and experiences. Therapist can also help you work through any feelings of isolation and loneliness.

4. Write about your experiences: Writing about your experiences can be a therapeutic way to process your feelings and help you feel less alone. Journaling, writing letters to yourself, or creating art can be healing to individuals.

5. Engage in self-care: Practicing self-care can help you feel more connected to yourself and less

isolated. Activities like exercise, meditation, or spending time in nature can be helpful for self-love and appreciation.

6. Educate yourself: Learning about the impact of sexual abuse and the experiences of other survivors can help you feel less alone and more understood. This can include reading books, attending workshops or seminars, or participating in online forums.

National Sexual Assault Hotline:
1-800-656-HOPE (4673)

CHAPTER 3

Grieving

Grieving is a challenging journey and there is no set timeline for healing after losing a loved one. In my life, I faced the devastating loss of multiple family members, one after another. The deaths of my five siblings in Africa due to poor health left me in a state of darkness and despair. Closure seemed out of reach, and I felt utterly alone. I literally had no one left to turn to. Many days I felt like giving up.

I was consumed by a constant ache in my heart, as if a part of me had been irreparably torn away. Each day felt like an uphill battle. I struggled to find meaning amid such immense loss, and the weight of loneliness grew heavier each day.

There were moments when I questioned my own strength and wondered if I could ever find the light at the end of the tunnel again. Grief had a way of distorting my perception of the world, casting a dark shadow over even the smallest glimmers of hope. It was as if I was trapped in a never-ending cycle of sorrow, unable to escape the grip of my emotions.

I couldn't comprehend why so many of my loved ones were taken from me. The weight of their absence consumed me and there were moments when I contemplated giving up. I questioned why I was left behind while they were gone. I prayed for strength just to make it through each day, sometimes struggling to find the will to move forward. I had to make the choice daily to choose between life over death.

The pain in my heart was overwhelming. Grief enveloped me, filling my days with sorrow and anger. I felt betrayed by the world and even questioned if God was punishing me. The course of my life seemed incomprehensible, but I had to find a way to navigate through the pain and confusion, for the sake of my children.

Grief can hit you like a ton of bricks and take the very last air out of your lungs. That sense of hollowing and an inability to breathe is real. When I thought of grief sometimes all I could think about were the empty seats at the table for the holidays. I constantly battled with the spirit of loneliness until I learned to find comfort in my creator. Grieving for me is an understatement. Words cannot fully capture the depth of grief that I experienced. No one can truly prepare you for this journey. While grieving, the idea of suicide sometimes seemed tempting and easy. I convinced myself that my children would understand if I chose that path. However, the thought of subjecting them to the same pain I knew so well as a motherless and fatherless child, overwhelmed me.

Feeling alone was one of the hardest aspects of my grief, even when surrounded by grieving family members and friends. Our pain may be shared, but each person's experience is uniquely their own. Recognizing this doesn't necessarily ease the difficulty of this time, but it is vital to be mindful of how we respond to these emotions and strive to find healthy ways to navigate the path o loss.

I turned to prayer, seeking forgiveness, guidance, and a new direction to overcome the pain and fears that consumed me. I am grateful for the opportunity to share my journey and hoping that we can all find healing and reclaim our voices to share our stories with the world.

7 WAYS TO COPE WITH GRIEF:

Grief is a natural and normal response to loss, and everyone experiences it differently. Here are some ways that people can cope with their grieving process:

1. Allow yourself to feel your emotions: It's important to acknowledge and accept your feelings, whether they are feelings of sadness, anger, guilt, or any other emotions.

2. Talk to someone: Consider talking to a trusted friend, family member, or therapist about your feelings and thoughts. Talking can help you process your emotions and work through your grief.

3. Write it down: Writing in a journal or expressing your feelings through creative writing can help you process your emotions and make sense of your experiences.

4. Seek support from a support group: There are support groups available for people who are grieving, which can provide a safe and supportive environment for you to share your experiences and emotions with others who are going through similar experiences.

5.   Practice self-care: Taking care of yourself physically and emotionally can help you manage the stress and emotions that come with grieving. This can include activities such as exercise, eating well, getting enough sleep, and taking time for yourself.

6.   Find meaning in the memories: Remembering the person you lost and honoring their memory, can help you find comfort and healing. You can create memorials, tell stories, or do activities that remind you of them.

7.   Seek professional help: If your grief is overwhelming and affecting your daily life, consider seeking the help of a mental health professional or a spiritual leader, who can provide you with additional support and coping strategies.

Remember, grief is a personal and individual experience, and there is no "right" or "wrong" way to grieve. It's important to be patient and kind to yourself as you work through your emotions and experiences. Extend grace to yourself.

CHAPTER 4

A Promise Fulfilled

O ne day, news reached me that my grandaunt was in town, visiting from the US. The excitement within me was overwhelming since I hadn't seen her since I was just a toddler. As soon as she laid eyes on me, she ran towards me and held me in a tight embrace, a hug that I hadn't felt since my mother's passing. Her warmth, love, and comfort filled my heart, creating an instant connection between us. Over the next few months, we forged an incredible bond and developed a beautiful relationship. She became the mother figure I had longed for, and the time spent with her became some of the best days of my life.

However, as the days passed, I learned that my grandaunt's visit was temporary, and she would soon be returning home to the United States. This realization saddened me, as I wished I could leave with her. To ease my worries, she promised me that she would come back for me and, in the meantime, work on processing my immigration documents to obtain a US travel visa. Holding onto her words, I patiently waited for the day when my dream of relocating to the US would become a reality.

During this waiting period, I found myself experiencing a deep longing to become a mother. Seeing my friends getting pregnant and starting families stirred a strong desire within me. I began to question whether I could have a child, as I had not become pregnant in any of my previous encounters. Yearning for motherhood, I fervently prayed for God's blessing to grant me the gift of a child.

Soon enough, I met a persistent man who showed a genuine interest in me. His persistence eventually led me into a relationship with him, hoping that he could fulfill my prayers of becoming a mother. After being together for some time, I discovered that I was finally pregnant with our son. I believed that my life would improve after becoming pregnant, but instead, I faced judgment and criticism from others. They advised me to consider abortion, warning that my life would be ruined. Fear crept in as I contemplated the possibility that my chances of coming to America to pursue the American dream had been shattered due to my pregnancy. People couldn't see beyond my circumstances, viewing me as a flawed pregnant girl from Africa, with hopes and dreams seemingly lost. It was a disheartening experience as I found myself questioning why God had granted me this blessing only to have it seemingly jeopardize my life-changing opportunity. However, I reminded myself that God was in control, and His plan would prevail in my life.

Shortly after learning of my pregnancy, my grandaunt discovered the news. Although upset, she remained determined to fulfill her promise of providing a better life for me in America. After a couple of months, my immigration documents were finally approved, and she arranged for me to travel to the United States to live with her. I am immensely grateful to the Almighty God for granting me this opportunity and for allowing my grandaunt to open her doors for me. Finally, I was blessed with the chance to offer my unborn son a better life than I had ever known growing up.

I vividly remember the day my grandaunt assured me, "I won't leave this country without you by my side." True to her word, she fulfilled her promises and unknowingly saved me from a path of uncertainty. Coming to America was a dream come true, a testament to God's plan for both me and my baby. I eagerly await the blessings that are yet unfolding in my life, knowing that God has a purpose for us. I am deeply thankful to my grandaunt for everything she has done, for being my rescuer, and for the love she has shown me. Thank you, Grandaunt. I love you from the depths of my heart.

CHAPTER 5

Embracing Motherhood and Navigating a New Life

Being a mother and an immigrant in the United States with not much education was very challenging. Here I am, this little country girl from Liberia now living in this huge city called Philadelphia, PA. It was very hard to start over from scratch let alone start over while pregnant. I experienced a severe culture shock because I looked and spoke differently from the people I was first exposed to here in America. I was once again silenced by my fear of not fitting in and starting over. I thought to myself, "how can I find and make this my new normal?" My fear and anxiety became more intense every time I went out into the community. All my life I had to fight just to fit in and never felt like I was good enough due to my unstable and traumatizing past.

Despite the challenges, I welcomed motherhood with an open heart when my newborn baby boy arrived just three months after settling in the United States. Although I felt unprepared for this new role, I cherished the opportunity and thanked God for entrusting me with the gift of motherhood. My son became the center of my universe, my heart overflowing with love for him. He was a true blessing from God, and I saw glimpses of myself reflected in his eyes. During this time, my in-laws played an instrumental role in helping me navigate the early stages of motherhood. Their guidance and support taught me invaluable lessons about caring for my baby and embracing my role as a mother. I am forever grateful for their presence and the profound impact they have had on my life.

God's divine plan continued to unfold as my son's father also had the opportunity to migrate to the United States, allowing us to raise our child together. I thanked God for granting us the chance to have a complete family, with both parents present to nurture and care for our baby boy. It was a blessing to witness our son grow and thrive in the loving environment we had created.

Three years later, our family was once again blessed when God bestowed upon us the gift of a beautiful daughter. She brought an abundance of joy and completed our little family. The day she entered this world was a moment I will never forget, etched deeply in my memory. She possesses a striking resemblance to me, both in physical appearance and in her fearless spirit. My daughter's boldness and her ability to speak her mind with unwavering confidence constantly remind me of the strength within her. I am grateful to God for the precious gift of my daughter and deeply admire her as God's gift to me.

As a mother, I faced numerous challenges and overcame many obstacles while building a new life in a foreign land. Yet, with each obstacle and every cherished moment spent with my children, I found the courage to embrace my role as a mother and the strength to push ahead. God's blessings were evident throughout this journey, and I am forever grateful for the love and joy my children have brought into my life. Together, we navigate the complexities of this world, united by the unbreakable bonds of family and the steadfast grace of God.

CHAPTER 6

My hopeless Fairytale

Being in love is a dream that every girl or every woman dreams of. We all want to be loved by our child's or children's father. This is something we pray for, but we often forget that to love someone else we must first love ourselves from within. However, if one doesn't know what true love is, one cannot give love. We could spend our entire life looking for love in all the wrong places. What is the definition of true love?

I was finally convinced that true love exists. When I first met my children's father, I knew he was Godsent. He courted me like I was a queen and treated me like no other man have ever shown me before. He gave me a reason to love and believe in love again. Finally, I found someone who made me feel complete. I was finally able to fill the voids of not having a complete family and a loving household. His love for me was that strong and powerful. I no longer felt invisible. He showed me what mature and masculine love looks like. Through him, I learned what it meant to have a man lead, provide, profess his love, and cover me as his partner.

I was on cloud nine and just when I thought our love couldn't get any better, I started to see the shift in our relationship. I thought his obsession with me was normal and that is how he shows his love. I thought his masculinity was very attractive and was how a man is supposed to lead. Until one day I started to realize that his obsession with me was control. If he gave me an order and I did not obey, I started to see his mean side. He just switched overnight, and everything caught me off guard. He started to argue nonstop and say disturbingly mean things to me that hurt me to my core. How can a man talk like this to a woman who births him two kids? How can he go from treating me like a queen to worse than an animal?

As I expressed earlier, when you haven't experienced real love, you don't really know what real love looks or feels like. So, anything that looks like love, we will find ourselves attracted to it because we don't know any better. We lack a healthy view and definition of love. My relationship with my children's father was great at first, but it cost me everything. I went through so much physical and emotional abuse in that relationship. I experienced so many things I am not proud of, but I am happy to be alive to tell my story.

The physical abuse I experienced could have taken my life and left my children motherless. Once again, this hurt became my norm and silenced me with fear of leaving and fear of starting over. Because I was so numb to the abuse, it became a normal lifestyle for both of us. For him, that was his love language to me, or so I thought. That was the way he knew how to speak to me because I allowed it. I endure those physical abuses for so long that it became so normal to me. What caught me by surprise was when he started to perform those same abusive acts outside of the home. When it was going on in the house, it was easy to cover up and I felt the need to still protect him. When the abuse got out of hand and he started to repeat it in public, that is when I knew I was in trouble, and it was getting out of control.

I had to find a way to escape and protect myself and my children. I took my babies and went to a friend's home whom I called a mother today. She helped me and my babies and provided a roof over our heads. This lady helped me so much with my children and provided an opportunity for us to start over from scratch.

I had no clue how I was going to survive as a single

mother of not one but two children. Two young babies, two and five years old. Both kids were in diapers, and I had to work so hard with no credit, and no bank accounts to myself. All the money I worked and received went straight to him and only he could cash it. I was mentally and emotionally crippled and only knew how to survive life with him. Even though it was turmoil and toxic, that's all I knew and that was my norm. How do I start over from scratch with two children? How can I survive with not even a penny to my name?

I just knew it wasn't going to be an easy task, but I was left with no choice. It was my time to either sink or swim. I thought having a man who was willing to be with me and take care of me and our children was true love. Having experienced physical and emotional abuse from people in my past, whom I thought should have loved me unconditionally but instead hurt me was my norm and the icing on the cake. I kept asking God to give me the strength to one day just leave because I never thought I could even escape and make it on my own with two young babies. However, to God be the glory. He always makes a way out of no way. Staying with my friend was the best decision I have ever made. She instructed me to stay by her home with the kids until I got on my feet and could survive on my own.

For my protection, I was instructed to get a restraining order against him so he could never get close to me and hurt me again.

From that day on I made up my mind to start a new chapter and I never looked back again after I closed that book of my life. I am so grateful for the people God placed in my life as my guardian angels who helped me along the way. Having the right tribe of people around you can be life changing. It really takes a village and a loving supportive community because no one can survive on an island alone.

CHAPTER 7

New Beginnings and Learning to Prioritize

S tarting over at my friend's house was a dream come true. God blessed us to the point where me and my children had our own room. After going through so much, I was happy to finally find my new normal. I was getting back to loving myself more and developing a healthier parenting relationship with my children. I believe when you are a better person you can love and parent even better.

During our time at my friend's house, I encountered a new tenant who was also renting from her. This remarkable man quickly became a close friend, displaying immense love and care for me and my children without any expectations in return. I was overwhelmed with gratitude that God had placed someone in our lives who willingly embraced the role of a father figure to my kids, even as just a friend. It was a novel experience for me to encounter a man who showed kindness without ulterior motives. As I observed his interactions with my children, I couldn't help but develop feelings for him. Despite my fears of opening my heart and diving into another relationship so soon, I realized that taking chances and hoping for the best is an integral part of discovering genuine love. Nevertheless, I recognized the need to tread cautiously and focus on my personal growth and the well-being of my children before fully investing in a romantic relationship.

While this new relationship began on a positive note and seemed to be headed in a promising direction, some things take time to fully comprehend. Before I knew it, the situation began to drain me emotionally, as my focus shifted towards protecting the other person rather than considering the needs of my children. It was during this time that God blessed me with my third daughter, whom I love dearly. However, throughout my pregnancy, I started to feel a decline in the support and love that was once present. Emotionally drained and filled with doubt, I questioned whether continuing with the pregnancy was the right decision.

I found myself constantly crying, asking God why I had to face such challenges again, especially after the turmoil I had endured just a few years prior. Now, with three children to care for, I was confronted with the unimaginable, making a decision I never thought I would have to make again.

In moments of desperation, I turned to prayer, seeking God's strength and guidance to navigate this difficult crossroads. Eventually, I felt a surge of inner strength, an assurance that God was by my side. With unwavering faith, I took a leap of faith, packing up our belongings and embarking on a new chapter. I had no money to my name and had to wait for my next paycheck, but I trusted that God's grace would sustain us through the transition.

As parents, we often fail to comprehend how profoundly our decisions impact our children. We may believe that we are doing the best we can, but it is crucial to consider our children's feelings and well-being in every decision we make. This realization hit home when we moved into our new apartment. While on the phone with our landlord, I found myself laughing at something he said. Little did I know, my middle daughter was observing me, and she turned to her brother and exclaimed, "Sam, mommy made the best decision ever!" Her words resonated deeply within me, reminding me of the tremendous weight our choices bear on our children's lives. It was a powerful moment. From then on, I vowed to prioritize my children's feelings and needs in every decision I made.

The transition to our new life was far from easy, but with God's unwavering presence and the support of friends, we navigated through the challenges. I am forever grateful to those friends who selflessly incorporated my children's activities into their own schedules, ensuring their well-being while I worked multiple jobs to provide for our needs. Words cannot express the depth of my appreciation for all they did for us, and their kindness will forever be etched in my heart.

Thank you all for being a part of our journey and standing by us during our times of struggle. Your love, support, and generosity have touched our lives in profound ways, and we will always cherish the memories we created together.

CHAPTER 8

Motherhood-A Saving Grace

Motherhood has not only saved my life, but it has also been the only relationship that has never failed me. Throughout my journey, there have been numerous moments when I found myself on the brink of giving up. The disappointments, setbacks, failures, and betrayals had taken a toll on me, and I felt drained both physically and emotionally. However, when I reflect on my own experience as a motherless child, I am reminded of the trauma and pain that accompanied it. I couldn't bear the thought of my children enduring the same cycle. I was determined to provide them with a different life—a life I never had but always wished for.

My children are my world, and I consider them to be God's greatest gifts to me. All I wanted was to be the best mother I could be for them. I was willing to go to great lengths, even if it meant working four different jobs with back-to-back shifts and sacrificing sleep to provide for our family. All I wanted was the American dream and to be able to gift my children the life that I wished for but never experienced myself.

Three years later, after juggling multiple jobs and piecing my life back together, I yearned to provide my growing children with a larger living space. However, as a single parent with a minimum wage salary and poor credit, the odds were stacked against me. Obtaining a mortgage seemed like an impossible feat. Despite these challenges, I decided to take a leap of faith, trusting in God's strength to guide me. Determined to increase my income, I took on a fifth job.

I worked tirelessly, hardly spending any time at home, and pushing myself to the brink of exhaustion. Finally, God answered my prayers. I had sacrificed everything to make it happen, but I was able to purchase our first home. A beautiful three-bedroom, two-and-a-half-bathroom townhouse in a wonderful suburban neighborhood in New Jersey. This new home provided my children with the opportunity to attend a better school in an excellent district. Although I was hardly home, with the nursing home becoming my primary residence, my children remained happy, and their happiness was all that mattered to me. We lived comfortably and peacefully in our new home, and I managed to cover all the bills on my own, ensuring the well-being of my babies.

Buying my own home was a dream come true, especially for a little girl from a small town called Lazelemai, where hope and dreams seemed distant. Despite my circumstances, I had managed to achieve a significant dream. There were moments when I contemplated giving up on myself and my children, believing that the world was against us. I felt unloved, unattractive, and unworthy of love. I reached my lowest point and even contemplated suicide. However, right on time, God intervened and saved me from myself. He led me through the darkest times, and if He could do it for me, He can do it for anyone.

For the first time in my life, I experienced true peace and happiness. Most importantly, I started to love myself like never before. This time, my self-love wasn't dependent on being in a relationship or the fear of being alone. I no longer made men the source of my happiness. Instead, I focused entirely on myself and my children's well-being and happiness.

As an immigrant mother with limited job experience, I understood that I needed to work harder than others to make life easier for myself and my family. I sought additional training and worked on improving myself in areas where I faced more challenges than others. As mentioned earlier, I hadn't completed my schooling back in Liberia, and I recognized the importance of furthering my education to achieve success in America.

I realized that going back to school was necessary if I wanted to secure a better future for my children and myself. With the support of my family and friends, I enrolled in night classes at a local community college. It wasn't easy juggling work, motherhood, and education, but I was determined to succeed.

Like so many immigrants, as a little girl coming from a third-world country living below the poverty line with no hope, I wanted to take advantage of the opportunity of being here in America as a blessing to change my life. I wanted to use this opportunity most people don't get to transform my life. Today, I want to help others who can relate to my story. I want my life to be a true testimony that there is hope and no one should ever give up on their dreams.

During those years of studying, I faced countless challenges and obstacles. There were days when I was so exhausted and doubt constantly flooded my mind. But every time I looked into my children's eyes; I found the strength to keep going. They were my motivation, my inspiration to persevere.

Just remember your circumstances are just temporary and not permanent. Your past does not determine or dictate who you are or what your future holds. Only if you let it. I am a true definition of what God can do in transforming our life. Mothers stay strong and keep the faith. We are all in this together. You are a walking miracle because whatever didn't break you was meant to build you. Keep building queens.

I am so blessed to live my life as a mother to my three beautiful children. I dedicate my life and this book to my three children: Samuel, Samantha, and Jamie. Today, my children are thriving. They are excelling in school, pursuing their passions, and dreaming larger than I did growing up. I couldn't be prouder of the young individuals they have become. And while I continue to work hard to provide for them, I also make sure to prioritize self-care and spend quality time with them. We have created beautiful memories together, overcoming the struggles and celebrating the victories as a family.

Motherhood has transformed my life in ways I never imagined. It has taught me that no matter how challenging life may be, there is always hope. It has shown me the strength that resides within me and the power of love to heal wounds and create a better future.

As I reflect on my journey, I am filled with gratitude. I am grateful for the opportunity to be a mother, to love and be loved unconditionally. Motherhood has saved me in more ways than one, and I will forever cherish this role as the greatest gift I have ever received.

Chapter 9

"Embracing The Future"
Acknowledging My Awesome Son

I want to take a moment to acknowledge my incredible son and firstborn, Samuel. You introduced me to the beautiful journey of motherhood when I thought it might never happen. Your arrival changed my life in ways I can never fully express. Through all the ups and downs, you have been my rock, standing by my side. I cannot begin to explain how much you have impacted my life.

Every decision I have made has been influenced by you and your sisters. I am grateful for the responsible and mature young man you have become and for the invaluable assistance you have provided in caring for your sisters. Your protective nature towards them fills my heart with love and gratitude. I remember how you made sure your baby sisters had food prepared and were safe while I was out working tirelessly to provide for us and keep a roof over our heads.

You had to grow up faster than most kids your age, shouldering the responsibility of taking care of your siblings while still being a child yourself. I cannot thank you enough for all that you have done.

I will never forget the time when our landlord was about to raise the rent payment on our apartment, and I contemplated finding another place for us to move. Your sisters were too young to understand the situation, but you looked me in the eyes and said, "Mommy, can you work more jobs so that we don't have to move again? I love my school, and I don't want to leave my friends. Please, mommy, I don't want to move again. I will be a good kid and take care of Samantha and Jamie, so you can work in peace. We will be fine, mommy." Your words touched my soul, and I replied, "Okay, Sam, I will see what I can do." Tears welled up in my eyes, but I fought back the emotions, as I always did in tough times, so you and your sisters wouldn't see me cry.

As a parent, all I want is to see my children happy and at peace. I made it my priority to make sacrifices so that we could live a happy and comfortable life. While writing this chapter, I am in awe of how a young child like you could express such touching sentiments. But then again, I'm not surprised because I had placed you and your sisters in challenging situations. I was glad that you spoke up for yourself and your sisters, especially when they couldn't articulate their needs at such a young age. I took your advice to heart and did exactly as you asked me to do for us. I took on a fifth job, working tirelessly day in and day out with different agencies. It wasn't easy, but with God's strength and your words of encouragement, I found the motivation to work even harder each day. So, thank you, my son.

As I write this book, I ask for your forgiveness for any poor decisions I made in the past that may have affected you. A few years ago, you expressed your thoughts of running away from home at the tender age of nine because you were unhappy with some aspects of our home life. Hearing those words from you, my son, broke my heart. I am grateful that God guided you to stay, as I don't know what I would have done if you had left. My heart wasn't strong enough. Thank you for choosing to stay by my side. I am truly sorry for everything I put you through. At times, I was overly protective and didn't allow you to experience things and figure them out on your own. You repeatedly told me,

"Mommy, I'm not your little baby anymore. Please let me be a man like my friends." I wanted to protect you at all costs because you protected me more than you'll ever know.

I apologize for how that made you feel, as you expressed to me before I had the opportunity to write this book. I hope that by taking your advice, I can make you proud. Thank you so much for being my awesome son. I love you with all my heart, and I pray that you continue to flourish in life, guided by God towards all your dreams and aspirations. Thank you for breaking generational patterns and becoming a trailblazer as the first college graduate in our family. We are immensely proud of you and the remarkable achievements you continue to accomplish, setting a path for your siblings to follow. I love and appreciate you, my awesome son. Thank you, and I love you. -----

UNMUTED

To My Beautiful Daughter, Samantha

To my beautiful first daughter, Samantha, I want to express my deep gratitude for the joy you bring into my life each day. Your presence is a true blessing, especially considering the circumstances surrounding your arrival. After experiencing a heartbreaking miscarriage, I had a dream of you that brought immense happiness. It felt so real, but God decided to take you back at that time. However, exactly one year later, you came back to me. God saw the pain and longing in my heart after losing you, and He brought you back to me as a double gift and an answered prayer.

You are truly a special gift that God had planned for me at His own perfect time, as neither the miscarriage nor the birth control I was on could prevent your existence. Samantha, I know that our mother-daughter relationship has had its challenges, but you have always reminded me of your desire for a strong bond between us. I have always longed for that too, to make up for the lost time. Despite the circumstances, our love has always remained a powerful connection between us.

I must confess that at times, I have been overly protective of you and your siblings. My intentions were always rooted in love. I am glad that you have discovered your identity and grown into a mature young lady. I am incredibly proud of the beautiful queen you are becoming as you transition from a princess. I now understand that you are no longer a baby, and I need to allow you the space to grow, trusting that I have done my best as your mother. You are an amazing daughter, and I love you more than words can express. Please forgive me for my shortcomings and for not always meeting your expectations as your mother. My prayer is that God protects and guides your every step toward the desires of your heart. Thank you for choosing me to be your mom. I adore you, my beautiful daughter Samantha.

To My Adorable Daughter, Jamie

I want to express my deepest gratitude to my adorable daughter, Jamie, for the endless love you bring into my life every single day. You are a true angel, and I am eternally grateful for your presence. Your arrival came at a time when I was going through so much, and I needed a miraculous shift to propel me forward. It was during this storm in my life that God blessed me with you, my third child. You represent my fresh start, as the number three symbolizes new beginnings. What I admire most about you is your unconditional love for others and your incredibly big heart.

One of my most cherished memories with you was when I underwent surgery and experienced immense pain. You stayed by my side throughout the ordeal. Even though I slept downstairs on the couch to ease my discomfort, you decided to sleep right next to me, holding my hands. You took care of me and helped nurture me back to health. I remember one day when the pain became unbearable, and tears streamed down my face, you started crying too. You said, *"Mommy, I don't want anything to happen to you. You didn't need this surgery. You are beautiful just the way you are."* Those words struck me deeply because you were right.

I couldn't understand why I had to undergo that surgery in the first place. Your wisdom, at such a young age of ten, advising me to love myself just the way I am, helped me immensely with my self-confidence.

You are truly one of a kind, my sweet and adorable daughter. Thank you for being my motivator and always reminding me of my worth. Whenever I doubted myself and questioned my value, you were always there to reassure me that I am more than enough. Words alone cannot express the depth of my gratitude for you. I pray that God blesses you abundantly and grants you all the desires of your heart. I love you, my adorable daughter.

CHAPTER 10

Taking a Leap of Faith

I t had been seven years since my last relationship, and I was at the peak of my life. I finally found power in my singleness and as a single mom. After so many failed relationships, setbacks, and disappointments, I wasn't interested in pursuing any more romantic relationships. I was tired of doing relationships my way and I wanted God to send me the right person at his divine time.

I had just reached a point where I was finally feeling free from my past hurts and relationship traumas. I now know what it feels like to be free and whole. I started dating myself and spending more time with my kids. I was becoming the best version of myself. I also took a leap of faith and followed my dream as a model and an actor. I always thought this wasn't possible for a girl like me migrating from Liberia. I wasn't what Americans would consider commercially beautiful. I was told by a couple of agents my complexion was too dark and I wasn't fit to be a model on their roster. However, it gave me more courage to prove them wrong and to power my way through creating my own lane as a dark skin model. I never took no for an answer. I always believe people's NO to me is God's way of telling me not right now or He has something better in store for me.

I finally did it. A couple of months later I was able to sign with an agent who embraced me and my unique beauty. She saw me and she added me to her roster of represented talents. This gave me such a boost of confidence. I was on fire and on top of the world. I was living my life like it was golden. The only thing that was missing from my life was a romantic partner. However, as I stated earlier, I was no longer searching but wanted to be prepared for when he came. I wanted to be ready to embrace love and possibly give it another chance.

One day I received a random call from a former coworker. We always saw each other in passing at our former job but there was no romantic attraction there. So, I was a little surprised when I got a call from this man out of the blue for the first time expressing his attraction to me. I was so caught off guard but deep down inside I admired his boldness. He at least piqued my interests, and I took him up on his offer to go out on a date. We started hanging out as friends and I was captivated by his energy as my friend, but he wanted more. He was very intentional and bold about wanting a family and marriage again. The icing on the cake that really had me impressed was when he told me about his relationship with God. I always wanted a man who is God-fearing and family oriented. So far, he was checking all my boxes and assuring me that he could see me as his wife. He told me that I was the wife he had been waiting and praying for all these years.

I finally gave in and gave love another chance. I was no longer going to lead with fear and doubts. I was ready to take a leap of faith or so I thought. I accepted his offer to be his girlfriend but by the time I blinked, he wanted me to be his wife. I didn't know how to feel. I was excited to be his wife but nervous about how fast he was moving. I barely had time to catch my breath or think of my answer. So, I just went with the flow, hoping this was God's will. What really tugged on my heart was when he went to church with me and after the second visit, he decided to join the church. I remember everyone at the church being so happy for me. We all thought God answered my prayers. Not only did this man want to marry me but he was ready to join my church home and get counseling from our pastor. Some of my loved ones were concerned at how fast he was moving but were still happy for us because he was including God in our relationship. So, I felt safe to let my guard down and allow him to love me. He did everything that was required to become a full member of the church. He was doing everything that I had proposed and wanted from a husband. He was proving himself that he was equipped to be the man I had been praying to come into my life.

One day we went to church as usual, and he was getting his certificate of completion for his new member class. I was so proud of him. When he went up to receive his certificate, I knew something was strange because he took the mic and started thanking everyone which is not usual for new members. To my surprise, he called me up to the front of the church to thank me in front of everyone. It was such a special gesture, but I was not prepared to be called out. I was not looking my best and was ready to rush back to my seat. However, before I could turn around to sit down, he proceeded to get down to one knee and ask for my hand in marriage. I was so numb and lost for words. All I could say was "Yes". As everyone jumped up and started cheering, I started to see families and friends appear out of nowhere. Although I was nervous, I felt like I was on top of the world.

It is finally happening. Everything that I have been praying and looking for in a partner was finally here. After the proposal and counseling from our pastor, I was ready to become his wife. Although it was romantic and everything I prayed for, something still felt off and unsettled. I wasn't sure if it was just my nerves, fear, or just the marriage jitters brides always get before they get married. God, am I doing your will? I prayed but the answers weren't clear. So, I thought I had nothing to lose by just taking a chance on love again.

Sometimes when we move at our own pace, it doesn't feel like peace or comfort. We may even try to convince ourselves that we are in fact doing or making the right decision. We convince ourselves that God has answered our prayers. Sometimes people will come into your life for their own motives and will do everything that you proposed and desire. Giving you reasons to believe that they are all in and ready to make this lifetime commitment. Even if it requires them to grow out of their comfort zone, they will quickly adjust due to the benefits they will gain.

After experiencing failed relationships, my fiancé vowed not to have any more divorces in his life. He promised me that I was his final relationship and the answer to his prayers. All his prior relationships prepared him to be the best husband for me, he said. *"Divorce would never be an option for us."*

I found confidence in his word and trusted where God was taking us. Words are very powerful to me. So even when we went through hard times and had disagreements, I never felt like it was going to get to that point of divorce. I really believed that this man really loved me and was God-sent. I always reflected on those words that he said to me to find comfort in my marriage. He said, *"Whatever we go through, we will work them out through thick and thin."*

If only I knew what I was getting myself into. I didn't find out until after we got married that he was still not healed and was still bitter about his prior relationship. He still had emotional and financial damages from his past relationships that I didn't know about until after we exchanged our vows. I had no idea I was going to be used as a stepping stool for him to level up. I was paying the price for what his past hurts cost him. When people are damaged and unhealed, it's inevitable that they will inflict hurt and pain on others. Like the saying goes, "hurt people hurt people." That was the reality of my marriage and my life. It's like I blinked my eyes and my life changed overnight. I felt like I was in a twilight zone and was living with a stranger. I wanted to escape my reality.

I did everything to try and save my marriage. One of the biggest sacrifices was selling my home I had worked so hard to earn for me and my kids. However, he didn't feel comfortable living in the house I had before him. For a fresh start in our marriage, I sold my prior house, and we got a bigger home for our new family. I thought our marriage would have blossomed from there, but it got worst. As our life began to change for the better, his behavior started to change for the worst. His patience started to decrease towards me. I felt like I was being tolerated and no longer celebrated.

What happened to the man who professed his love for me in front of our entire congregation, families, and friends? Was I being pranked? Who is this man that I am living with?   He was no longer practicing the fruit of the spirit towards me as his wife. Whatever happens to, "Love is patient, Love is kind." You get the picture. I was furious. This man came into myself and children's lives and interrupted everything I worked so hard to build by myself. I started to feel like I was married to a stranger. God, what have I done wrong? Did I make a huge mistake?

My home which was once so warm, and loving was now cold and uncomfortable. I felt like I was living in a prison. Captive to my thought and muted once again by my pain and betrayals. Just when I thought it couldn't get any worst. He was now starting to leave our home unannounced for days and even sometimes weeks at a time. I soon learned he was staying at hotels when he was away from home. A year later, one morning when I turned to my husband to have a casual conversation, he told me something that I was not expecting at all. He looked me in the eyes and told me he wanted a divorce and would leave this time for good. At this moment I felt numb and lost for words.

Whatever happened to "no matter how bad it gets we will always fix it despite the storms." What happened to our vows? Where was this coming from and was it that bad? We had no infidelity issues, no abuse, or anything that would justify us getting a divorce. At least not to my knowledge. Now he wants to throw in the towel and give up on our marriage just like that? All he could say was he had been thinking about divorce for a while but didn't know how to tell me.

THE TRUTH HURTS

When a person has mentally, emotionally, and physically checked out of a relationship, there's nothing you can do to change that. Never allow anyone to tell you they don't want to be with you more than once. When someone shows you, their true colors believe them and don't act color-blind due to your love and desires. I kept holding on to the empty promises that I got at the beginning of our marriage that no longer served me. I kept fighting because I didn't believe in divorce, and I wasn't ready to let it go. I felt like I was a wife first and I had the responsibility to fight for my marriage and not give up so soon. No matter how hard I fought for our marriage, all he could say in his defense was "you are going to thank me for leaving." I didn't understand what he meant by that, but I knew that I would soon find out. I was in a downhill battle to save my marriage by myself.

My thoughts at the time were, "my whole life was once again ruined." I couldn't believe what was happening. I wish that I could just wake up from this bad dream. I quickly realized that this wasn't a dream and I had to face the reality of my life. The next day after our initial divorce conversation, he told me he already filed for a divorce. I thought he was just being petty, but I came to find out it was true according to the filing date that was on the paper. This all happened while he was still living in our marital home. After he dropped this load on me, he had the audacity to move out and get his own apartment. Left all the mortgage and bills on me with no financial assistance. All resulted in me having to take on a second job just to survive, make ends meet, and pay for a divorce attorney. To my surprise, he had already checked out of our marriage and had his new life all mapped out without my children and me in the picture. I could not wrap my head around him making all these selfish decisions in such a short time.

When someone comes into your life with a mission and that mission has been fulfilled you will begin to see a declining shift in the relationship because the season has ended. Often time we try to hold on to relationships when the season is over, and they no longer serve a purpose. I know it's hard to wrap our minds around these hurtful circumstances, but we can't save relationships that no longer serve us and our purpose.

The signs and red flags are always there, we are just the last to admit to them. I should have known that we were in a rush to go nowhere. I felt in my spirit something was off because of how fast he was moving from dating to a proposal to marriage. Now looking back, it all made sense. I wanted to be loved and to have a complete family so badly that I ignored the red flags. Just because someone involves God, that doesn't mean it's of God. The wolf in sheep's clothing is an understatement for me. From the day we exchanged our vows, I felt a huge shift that I couldn't make sense of, but I kept believing in my marriage and trusting that God would bring clarity.

RECIA KABBAH

LESSON LEARNED

I have learned from my mistakes, and I am more aware and discerning about whom I should give my heart. Many people look at strong independent women as stepping stools and expect us to carry the whole world with their burdens on our shoulders. I had to accept the fact that I was not okay and that I could not walk around like I'm a superwoman. I was hurting and I felt alone and lost. I didn't know whom to turn to because I was embarrassed and ashamed of my divorce. I allowed the pain of my divorce to silence and isolate me because I was running away from my reality and didn't want constant reminders from others. So, I decided to suffer in silence. The only one I could cry out to was God. Although I kept a poker face and masked my pain with a smile, I was hurting. I had to keep pushing forward for the sake of my children. They were my why and my motivation to not give up on myself.

Divorce taught me many lessons. Looking back, now I can truly say that I am very grateful to God for choosing me to have this experience because it was necessary for my evolution. I kept repeating unhealthy cycles of relationships because I didn't know how to love, or how to be loved, and didn't know what a healthy marriage looks like. I didn't have examples of healthy relationships or marriages growing up. I had to learn through my own trials and errors. Like me, there are so many people who stay in unnecessary and unhealthy relationships because of their fear of being alone. We desire to have a complete family at any cost, even if it cost us ourselves and peace of mind.

I am very private and due to my upbringing; I was taught to never air my personal business outside of the home or let anyone see my struggles. So, in telling my story, this is a huge leap of faith for me. I've learned my mission and purpose on this earth are bigger than mine. I want to bring awareness to the power of being single. To have the boldness to be transparent with my story so that others who can relate can learn from my mistakes and know they're not alone in surviving setbacks, betrayal, and the death of a divorce. We can rewrite our stories and find strength in our failures to push forward to share our testimonies.

CHAPTER 11

Healing from a Divorce

G oing through a divorce can be a painful and challenging experience. However, it does not have to define the rest of your life. With time, patience, and the right mindset, you can heal from your divorce and open yourself up to love again. In this chapter, we will explore some strategies to help you heal and move on from your divorce. Divorce is not just the end of a marriage, it's the end of a life that you've built with someone you thought would be yours forever. It's the loss of your dreams, hopes, and future plans. It's a very heart-breaking experience that can leave you feeling broken and shattered. But despite the darkness and pain, there is still hope and a future after the death of a divorce. There is a chance for you to rise from the ashes of your divorce and start your new beginning. Let's dive into the emotional and compelling journey of healing from divorce and finding love again.

1. Give yourself time to grieve: The first step to healing is acknowledging and accepting the loss. It's normal to feel a range of emotions like anger, sadness, guilt, and confusion. Allow yourself to feel these emotions and grieve the loss of your marriage. Cry, scream, or punch a pillow if you must. It's okay to feel like you're falling apart because you are falling. Your life has changed, and it's okay to take the time to process it all.

It's important to acknowledge your emotions and allow yourself time to process your feelings. Don't try to rush through the healing process or ignore your emotions, as this can interrupt the healing process.

2. Seek support: Going through a divorce can feel isolating and lonely, but you don't have to go through it alone. Surround yourself with supportive friends and family members who can offer a listening ear and a shoulder to lean or cry on. You

3. may also consider seeking professional support, such as a therapist, counselor, or spiritual leader, who can help you work through your emotions and provide guidance. This was very difficult for me to share because at first, I wasn't accepting the reality that I failed at my marriage and was going through a divorce. However, I had to change the way I viewed my

divorce. I had to realize that I am not a failure, but the marriage failed. When I accepted that and changed my view, I started my journey of healing from my divorce. Remember that healing from a divorce is a process, and it's normal to experience ups and downs along the way.

4. Practice self-compassion: Self-compassion is the practice of treating yourself with kindness and understanding, especially during times of suffering. It's easy to be hard on yourself during and after a divorce but being compassionate towards yourself is crucial for your emotional well-being. Give yourself permission to take care of your needs and prioritize your well-being. You've been through a lot, and it's okay to take things slow and be gentle with yourself. Recognize that divorce is a difficult experience and it's natural to struggle with feelings of loss, guilt, sadness, and loneliness.

5. Focus on self-care: Divorce can take a toll on your physical and emotional well-being, so it's important to take care of yourself during this time. Make sure you're eating a healthy diet, getting enough sleep, and engaging in regular exercise. Take time to do things that make you happy, whether it's reading a good book,

going for a hike, getting a massage, or taking a relaxing bath. Remember that you deserve to prioritize your own needs and wants, and it's okay to take things slow.

6.   Practice forgiveness: Forgiveness is an essential part of the healing process after a divorce. This doesn't mean that you must forget what happened or condone the behavior that led to the divorce, but it does mean that you release yourself from the burden of anger, bitterness, and resentment. Forgiveness is a gift you give yourself, and it can help you move on from the pain and hurt of the past.

6.   Be open to new experiences & Focus on the future: While it's important to acknowledge and process your emotions, it's also important to look ahead and focus on building a fulfilling future. This may involve setting new goals, exploring new interests, or making positive changes in your life.

After you've taken the time to heal and process your emotions, you may feel ready to start dating again. Be open to new experiences and try not to compare potential partners to your ex-spouse. Remember that each person is unique, and you may find someone who brings new joys and challenges to your life. It's also important to communicate your needs and boundaries in any new relationship and take things at a pace that feels comfortable for you. When you're ready, opening your heart to love again can be a scary but exciting journey. Love is a risk, but it's a risk worth taking. There is love after the death of your divorce.

Healing from divorce is a journey that's very emotional, challenging, and ultimately rewarding. It's an opportunity to rediscover yourself, find new passions, and create a new life that's even better than the one you had before. With time, self-compassion, support, forgiveness, and an open heart, you can rise from the ashes of your divorce and find love again. Remember, you are stronger than you think, and you deserve happiness.

CHAPTER 12

What is Manipulation?

Manipulation is a hurtful tactic that I have personally experienced and seen in many others, used by people to control and manipulate others for their own gain. It can take on different forms, including emotional manipulation, where one is made to feel guilty, and your emotions are used to control you. This kind of manipulation can be extremely damaging, leaving you feeling confused and doubting yourself.

Recognizing manipulation and understanding its impact is crucial in protecting ourselves and maintaining healthy relationships. I have found some helpful resources that can provide valuable insights into manipulation and how to deal with it, referenced at the end of this chapter.

Manipulation can be physical or involve threats, making you feel trapped and scared. If someone is manipulating you, it is important to ask for help and talk to someone you trust. We often blame ourselves and think we are doing something wrong in the relationship when that's not the case. You don't have to go through this alone, and you deserve to be treated with kindness and respect. Remember that you have the power to take back control of your life. Manipulation can take many forms, and it is not always easy to recognize. Some common types of manipulation include:

Emotional Manipulation: Emotional manipulation involves the use of emotions to control someone's behavior. This type of manipulation can take many forms, such as guilt-tripping, gaslighting, or love-bombing. Emotional manipulators may use tactics like withholding affection or giving silent treatments to get their way.

Persuasive Manipulation: Persuasive manipulation involve the use of persuasive tactics to influence someone's behavior or beliefs. This can include misrepresenting facts or using persuasive language to make an argument seem more compelling.

Covert Manipulation: Covert manipulation involves using subtle tactics to influence someone's behavior without their knowledge. This can include things like planting ideas in someone's mind or using subliminal messaging to influence their behavior.

Physical Manipulation: Physical manipulation involves using physical force or threats to control someone's behavior. This can include things like intimidation or using physical violence to get someone to do what you want.

Manipulation can have serious consequences for the person being manipulated. It can lead to feelings of confusion, guilt, and self-doubt, and it can make it difficult for people to trust others. Manipulation can also lead to abusive situations, particularly in cases where physical or emotional violence is involved.

To protect yourself from manipulation, it is essential to learn how to recognize the signs of manipulative behavior. Some common warning signs include feeling guilty or responsible for someone else's emotions, feeling like you are always in the wrong, or feeling like you can never do anything right. If you suspect that you are being manipulated, it is important to seek help from a trusted friend, family member, or professional.

Understanding the different types of manipulation and learning how to recognize the signs of manipulative behavior can help you protect yourself and prevent others from taking advantage of you. By being aware of manipulation and taking steps to protect yourself, you can live a healthier, happier, and more authentic life.

SIGNS OF MANIPULATION

If you suspect that someone is manipulating you into doing something, it's essential to be aware of the signs of manipulation and take steps to protect yourself. Here are some tips on paying attention to someone with manipulating behaviors:

- Recognize the signs of manipulation: Some common signs of manipulation include guilt-tripping, gaslighting, playing the victim, and withholding information. If someone is using these tactics to get what they want, it's a sign that they may be trying to manipulate you.

- Trust your instincts: If you feel uncomfortable or uneasy around someone, it's essential to trust your instincts. Pay attention to how the person makes you feel, and if something doesn't feel right, it's best to proceed with caution.

- Set boundaries: Setting clear boundaries is crucial when dealing with manipulative people. Let the person know what you are and are not comfortable with and be firm in your boundaries.

- Be assertive: It's important to be assertive when dealing with manipulative people. Let them know that you won't tolerate their behavior and that you will not be manipulated.

- Seek support: If you're dealing with someone who is manipulating you, it can be helpful to seek support from a trusted friend or family member. They can offer you a different perspective and help you navigate the situation.

Remember, it's important to prioritize your own well-being and safety when dealing with manipulative people. If you feel like you're in danger or the situation is escalating, don't hesitate to seek professional help or involve law enforcement.

References:

Braiker, H. B. (2004). Who's Pulling Your Strings? How to Break the Cycle of Manipulation. McGraw-Hill Education.

Simon, G. K. (2016). In Sheep's Clothing: Understanding and Dealing with Manipulative People. Parkhurst Brothers Publishers Inc.

Forward, S. (1997). Emotional Blackmail: When the People in Your Life Use Fear, Obligation, and Guilt to Manipulate You. HarperCollins Publishers.

Marshall, P. (2015). Covert Emotional Manipulation Tactics: How Manipulators Take Control in Personal Relationships. CreateSpace Independent Publishing Platform.

National Domestic Violence Hotline. (2021). Manipulation and Relationships. Retrieved from https://www.thehotline.org/2018/07/05/manipulation-and-relationships/

CHAPTER 13

You are not what people label you...
Overcoming "Stupidity Labels"

Have you ever been called "stupid," "dumb," or "unintelligent"? Have you ever felt like you don't know enough, or that you don't fit in with your peers? If so, you may be experiencing the effects of trauma from the "stupidity label." Growing up and even as an adult, I am constantly fighting against the negative and insulting labels others placed on me, based on their own insecurities.

Based on reading Schussler-Fiorenza's article on *"Stupidity label"*, I have learned the many ways the "stupidity label" can impact your life, from self-doubt and low self-esteem to social anxiety and depression. How trauma affects the brain and the body, and how you can use this knowledge to heal yourself. To overcome the trauma of feeling stupid we must include identifying negative self-talk, reframing our beliefs about intelligence, and building self-compassion and resilience. Practical strategies for dealing with situations that trigger your trauma, such as public speaking, academic tests, or social gatherings. To cultivate a growth mindset, we must find our own unique strengths and talents because that is also where our power lies.

Whether you've experienced the "stupidity label" as a child, a teenager, or an adult, you can move beyond it and reclaim your sense of worth and belonging. With empathy, humor, and practical guidance, it offers a roadmap to healing that can benefit anyone who has ever felt like they don't know enough or don't fit in.

Moving on from the trauma of being called names like "stupid," "dumb," or "unintelligent" and never feeling like you fit in can be a challenging process. However, it is possible to overcome this trauma and live a fulfilling life.

Here are some key things to keep in mind as you work to heal labels and low self-esteem:

1. Acknowledge your feelings: It's essential to recognize the emotions that come up when you think about, or experience situations related to the trauma. Allow yourself to feel these emotions and acknowledge that they are valid.

2. Seek support: Talking with a trusted friend, family member, or therapist can provide a safe and supportive environment to process your feelings and work through your trauma.

3. Reframe your thoughts: Recognize that negative self-talk and beliefs about your intelligence can be a result of the trauma. Reframe these thoughts with positive and empowering messages.

4. Practice self-care: Make sure to prioritize self-care in your life. This can include activities like exercise, meditation, or spending time in nature.

5. Cultivate a growth mindset: Adopting a growth mindset can help you focus on learning and growth instead of fixed notions of intelligence.

6.   Take action: Finally, take action towards your goals and pursue your interests. This can help build confidence and a sense of purpose.

Remember, healing from trauma is a process that takes time, patience, and self-compassion. With effort and support, it is possible to move on from the trauma of being called names and never feeling like you fit into the box and limits others place on you.

References for "stupidity label":

Schussler-Fiorenza, R. (2002). The stupidity label. In S. M. Miller & L. L. Finley (Eds.), Speaking truth to power: A reader on Christian social ethics (pp. 240-247). Oxford University Press.

CHAPTER 14

Unmuted & No Longer Silenced by My Pain

The weight of our pain can be crushing, and we may feel like we're drowning in a sea of silence. But what if we could break free from the grip of our pain and rise above it? What if we could unmute our voices and shatter the silence that keeps us trapped? I want us to explore the power of being unmuted and no longer silenced by our pain.

What if I tell you, we all can find our power in speaking up. Silence can be a prison and speaking up can be the key to freedom. When we break the silence and share our pain, we take the first step towards healing. We may feel vulnerable and exposed, but we also open ourselves up to the possibility of connection, empathy, and understanding. Speaking up can be a liberating release, a way to shed the burden of our pain and start a new chapter in our lives. I am freeing myself by standing in my truth and transforming my mess into my message by writing my story of how I became unmuted. I am standing boldly now more than ever before in taking my power back and rewriting my story. I am now ready to change the narrative and tell my story now that I am free and unmuted.

In our journey of self-discovery, it's important to own our truth. Despite the good, the bad, and the ugly. It's our journey, it's our story. To be unmuted, we must first own our truth. This means facing our pain and trauma without running and taking responsibility for our healing journey. It's a journey of self-discovery, of uncovering the hidden corners of our hearts and minds and acknowledging the truth of our experiences. Owning our truth also means recognizing our resilience, strength, and courage in the face of adversity. It's a powerful reminder that we are survivors, not victims. It's a constant reminder that we are more than conqueror through God who fights all our battles.

Being unmuted requires vulnerability, the courage to be seen and heard. It's not easy to let down our walls and show our true selves, but it's necessary for healing and growth. Vulnerability invites connection, empathy, and understanding. It's a way to let others know that they are not alone, and to create a space for healing and support.

UNMUTED

To use my pain to find my power to create change, I first had to find my voice. Being unmuted means finding our voice and using it to speak up for ourselves and others. It's a powerful tool for creating change and making a difference in the world. Our scars are our mark we leave in this world. We can use our scars to have an impact on others through our testimony. Our voices have the power to raise awareness, inspire action, and create positive change. It's a way to take back control and advocate for us and others.

This journey has taught me so much about life and how a single decision could change one's entire life and trajectory. I do not take for granted what God has done for me. There were so many days I felt like giving up on myself and throwing in the towel. After all the turmoil I've been through, I had many great reasons that would justify my decision for doing so. Instead, I found beauty in my ashes and transformed everything that was meant to break me and allowed it to build me up. Through God's glory and direction, I allowed my brokenness to help me become a better version of myself, Recia 2.0.

I was able to use what could have been my downfalls to inspire me to make better choices. When I look back on my life, I see pain, mistakes, and heartaches. When I look in the mirror, I see strength, learned lessons, and pride in myself. I heard that not speaking on things just to keep the "peace" is a trauma response. When you do this, you disrespect your boundaries. No matter what, keep taking up space and use your voice to inspire others.

It's time to celebrate our healing as we bask in the joy of our transformation. Being unmuted and no longer silenced by our pain is a celebration of our healing journey. It's a reminder of our resilience, strength, and courage in the face of adversity. It's an opportunity to embrace the joy of transformation and to celebrate the person we've become. We may still carry scars and wounds, but we can also celebrate our growth, our newfound confidence, and our ability to rise above our pain.

I have learned to live without regrets or trade my life for anyone else's, because everything I've experienced made me the relentless woman that I am today. I am learning how to love, embrace and inspire myself as I continue to help others through their struggles and challenges. I want you to know that you can push through and overcome traumatic things.

My goal is to be the voice for the voiceless and to bring awareness to the power of standing in our truth. I want others to be able to own their mess boldly and learn from it.

Be bold enough to no longing live in fear and allow pain to keep us muted. I have also learned to love myself more and accept all my flaws and insecurities that were once holding me back and keeping me silenced. I have also learned how to love those who did not deserve my love. I have come to understand that people cannot give what they don't have or possess. In other words, they can't love others if they don't even know how to love themselves. So instead of being so quick to judge others I have come to accept and embrace everyone's flaws and all. I have learned to not get caught up with putting my expectations on others that they can't meet. When we start to put expectations on others, we will always find ourselves disappointed and hurt because someone has failed to be what we expect of them.

Understanding that your happiness is no one else's responsibility but your own. Also holding yourself accountable for your own actions is in your control. I am learning how to love and embrace myself more and more each day. I am now ready to submit everything to God that is both in and out of my control. I will never look back at the things that I have endured as a setback because they were all part of the process to prepare me for my comeback. In every situation staying positive is another way to moving forward and learning from your own experiences. You must know that there is a reason why God has you on this earth, and the purpose must be fulfilled in His own timing.

People come in our lives for many different reasons knowingly and unknowingly. Some people come to teach us a lesson and some are to remind us of who we are as a blessing. All of these are for us to embrace life's greatest blessings.

Being unmuted and no longer silenced by our pain is a journey of self-discovery, vulnerability, and transformation is empowering. This is your reminder that your voice matters, and your experiences are valid. This is an invitation to own our truth, embrace vulnerability, find our voice, and celebrate your healing.

CHAPTER 15

Forgiveness

Forgiveness is powerful! One of the most difficult challenges was forgiving my loved ones who hurt me deeply. It was especially hard to forgive those whom I never expected to hurt me. However, with the grace of God and His mercy, I found the strength to forgive my offenders.

I realized that I had to learn to love and accept people for who they are and where they are in their own journey of healing and self-discovery. If they are still wounded, they may unintentionally inflict their pain on others, especially those closest to them. Forgiveness is not just for the benefit of the offenders; it is primarily for us. It allows us to reclaim our power from those who have hurt us and attempted to break us.

To all those who entered my life with ill intentions and tried to break me, I want to express my gratitude. I am thankful for the lessons that our situations have taught me. Through these experiences, I have truly discovered my authentic self and learned that not everyone is deserving of my love. Not everyone understands the importance of being loved and how to reciprocate it.

I have come to understand that some individuals can be self-righteous and unaware of the pain they cause to those who genuinely love and care for them. Today, I stand here because I have forgiven myself and everyone who has hurt me in any way, shape, or form. The moment I realized that I am worthy and deserving of God's best, I set myself free. As Michelle Obama says, 'When they go low, we go high.'

Reflecting on my life, I realized that there were moments when it seemed like the world was against me. I carried immense pain and hurt within me, allowing it to fester. Additionally, I never properly grieved the loss of my mother, father, and two older siblings, which left a void that burdened my heart for a long time. While those pains and voids will always remain internally, I have learned to rely not on my own understanding, but to acknowledge the Lord in all my ways and let Him direct my path and provide me with strength.

I no longer let my past hurt and disappointments hold me back from living a fulfilling life and experiencing love again. I have embraced life to the fullest and learned to live in the present moment. I understand the importance of reciprocity and surround myself with those who embrace and celebrate me. It is vital to go only where we are celebrated, not merely tolerated. I choose to tolerate only reciprocity. It is essential to gracefully exit unhealthy situations that no longer serve us without harboring resentment, anger, or bitterness. Instead, I find peace within myself and grant permission to move on to the next chapter of my life. I forgive myself for any past wrong decisions and use those mistakes as valuable lessons to grow and shape the person I aspire to be. I know that I am enough.

While no one can fully comprehend my pain and suffering without having walked in my shoes, I firmly believe that God has a greater purpose for me on this earth, a purpose that I have yet to fulfill. God is just beginning His work in me, and I am excited to follow His lead, unapologetically being myself. I will continue to grow and strive to become a better person while embracing all that life has to offer.

I have learned to accept failure as a natural part of life. Nobody is perfect, and making mistakes is inevitable. It is crucial to embrace failure as an opportunity for growth and learning.

Our failures do not define who we are or determine our potential. Kindness and compassion are values I hold dear. Everyone is fighting their own battles, and by showing kindness and understanding, we can make a significant difference in their lives. Moreover, effective communication is essential. Expressing our thoughts and feelings in a constructive and respectful manner is crucial for maintaining healthy relationships. Bottling up our pain and suffering in silence only prolongs our hurt and prevents us from finding healing and resolution. Sharing our pain and communicating can be a powerful form of release.

Persistence is another key lesson I have learned. If we desire something, we must work diligently and never give up. By staying persistent, we increase our chances of achieving our goals and dreams.

Lastly, I have learned to appreciate the small things in life. Life is filled with unexpected surprises and moments of joy that we often overlook. Taking the time to recognize and appreciate these moments makes life much more enjoyable and fulfilling.

Forgiveness can be a difficult and complex process, but here are some suggestions and healing exercises to forgive those who have hurt you:

Acknowledge your emotions: Before you can begin to forgive, it's important to acknowledge and process your emotions. This may involve expressing your feelings through journaling, talking to a trusted friend or therapist, or engaging in self-care activities that help you feel calm and centered.

Practice empathy: Try to put yourself in the other person's shoes and understand their perspective. This doesn't mean that you condone their actions, but it can help you understand why they may have acted the way they did.

Let go of resentment: Holding onto resentment can prevent you from moving forward and can lead to feelings of anger and bitterness. Instead, try to release your anger and resentment by practicing self-compassion and reminding yourself that you deserve to live a happy and fulfilling life.

Set boundaries: Forgiveness doesn't mean that you must forget or condone the behavior that hurt you. It's important to set boundaries that protect your well-being and prevent the person from hurting you again in the future.

Practice forgiveness: Forgiveness is a process that takes time and practice. You may not be able to forgive someone overnight, but by practicing forgiveness regularly, you can gradually let go of negative emotions and move towards healing.

Forgiveness is a personal decision, and there's no one-size-fits-all approach to forgiveness. It's important to be patient with yourself and to seek support from loved ones or a mental health professional if you're struggling to forgive. I also struggled with how to heal from unforgiveness if my offender never apologized. Am I the only one who struggles with this? I allowed this to block my happiness and healing for so long because I was waiting for an apology. That's where I went wrong. Even if your offender never chooses to apologize, it is you that must take your powerful back with or without an apology.

Here are some steps that helped me guide me through therapy to help me forgive the people who hurt me and never apologized:

1.   Focus on yourself: Forgiveness is ultimately about your own healing and letting go of negative emotions. Rather than waiting for an apology, focus on your own feelings and work towards releasing resentment and anger.

2.   Let go of expectations: While an apology can be a powerful tool for healing and reconciliation, it's not

always necessary for forgiveness. Try to let go of any expectations that the person will apologize and instead focus on your own healing process.

3. Practice empathy: Even if the person hasn't apologized, try to understand their perspective and the reasons why they may have acted the way they did. This doesn't mean that you condone their behavior, but it can help you let go of negative emotions and move towards forgiveness.

4. Reframe the situation: Try to see the situation from a different perspective and reframe it in a positive light. This can involve focusing on the lessons you've learned or the ways in which the situation has helped you grow and become stronger.

5. Seek support: Forgiveness can be a challenging process, and it's important to seek support from loved ones or a mental health professional if you're struggling to forgive. Talking through your emotions with someone else can help you gain clarity and perspective on the situation.

Remember that forgiveness is a personal decision, and it may take time and practice to let go of negative emotions.

Be patient with yourself and take things one day at a time. With time and effort, you can move towards forgiveness and healing.

Remember to keep praying, trusting, and believing in the Lord. No dream is too big for God. He is the creator of everything possible and impossible. There's no such thing as a dead dream. If you have life, you have the power to make anything you desire come true. Your dreams can only die if you allow it by not trying. I hope that my story can help you discover your passion and purpose. Thank you all so much for coming on this journey with me. I am truly grateful, blessed, and highly favored. To God be the glory.

CHAPTER 16

The Gift of No and Dealing with Guilt

Learning to say no can be very difficult but it's a powerful gift to give yourself. So many of us are people pleasers and struggle with prioritizing ourselves. This was very challenging for me, and I had to use the gift of no for my self-care. Understand your priorities and commitments and evaluate whether saying yes to a request aligns with them. Saying no to something that doesn't align with your priorities is a way of honoring your time and energy.

Also, it's important to be honest with yourselves because you're nobody's doormat. If you need to say no, be honest about your reasons. You don't have to make excuses or justify your decision. Honesty is usually appreciated and respected. Little do you know, people may not like being told no because of selfish reason but they will respect honesty. So be honest with yourself first and to others. Remember you must train others how to treat and respect you.

If you're unable to say yes to a request, offer alternatives that could be helpful. This shows that you're willing to help in some way, even if you can't meet their original request. Most importantly, remember that saying no is not being selfish, self-centered, or mean. You have the right to prioritize your own needs and set boundaries. Practice self-compassion and let go of any guilt or shame associated with saying no. Saying no can be uncomfortable if you're not used to it. Practice saying no in a kind and respectful way. This can help you build confidence and feel more comfortable in your decision to say no.

Often, when I have said yes in the past out of guilt, I felt like I was being taken advantage of and I felt used. I had to acknowledge the emotions that I was experiencing and try to understand why I felt used. We must reflect on our experiences and identify the situations whenever we feel like we're being taken advantage of. Most importantly we must communicate how we feel to set boundaries and prevent this from happening again.

Instead of feeling guilty, try to reframe your perspective and focus on the positives. Recognize that being in the position to help others is a gift and a blessing. Think about the impact you have made on others' lives and focus on the good that you have accomplished. However, please set boundaries if you feel used by others. Learn to say no when you feel that you're being taken for granted and communicate your needs to others. It's important to talk to someone you trust about your feelings, and this could be a friend, family member, or therapist. Discussing your emotions can help you gain perspective and find a way to move forward.

Taking care of yourself is essential when you're feeling guilty or overwhelmed. Make time for activities that bring you joy, such as exercising, reading, or spending time in nature. Remember that it's okay to prioritize yourself and set boundaries to protect your own well-being.

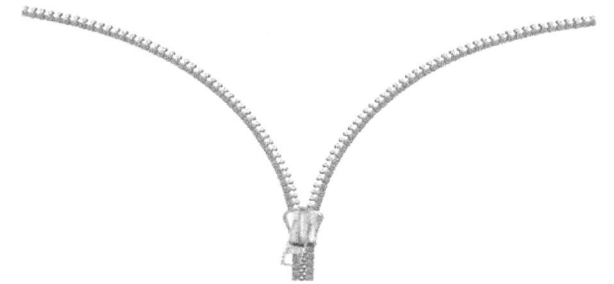

CHAPTER 17

RECIA 2.0

I am incredibly grateful for the present moment and the opportunity to celebrate my NOW. As I embark on writing my book and pursue my dream of running my business, RekaBoutique, in this new year, I am filled with anticipation and excitement. Starting this business has not only been a source of mental and spiritual growth for me but has also allowed me to bless other women by helping them look and feel fabulous. It's a fulfilling experience to live out my dream as an entrepreneur and inspire others to embrace their own beauty and self-confidence.

This venture came at the perfect time in my life, providing solace and strength as I navigate through the challenges and life-changing experience of my divorce. God has truly turned my pain into something beautiful, and I am emerging as a stronger and more empowered version of myself.

In this new chapter of my life, I am determined to travel and fully immerse myself in all that life has to offer while living my best life. I am excited about the direction God is leading me, as He has already opened doors and taken me to new heights I never imagined. I have gained a deeper understanding of the importance of trusting God and His process. Often, setbacks are merely setups for comebacks. On this journey, we encounter various obstacles and valley experiences that serve to shape and prepare us for the mountain peaks we will eventually conquer. Our testimonies are born from the tests we face.

I am finally breaking free from silence and reclaiming my power. This journey requires continuous renewal to elevate and transform into a higher standard of greatness. Never underestimate the power within you and the potential you possess. We often undermine ourselves and our abilities due to fear of failure. However, if we continue to trust in God, He will never leave or forsake us. Every experience that I have gone through has played a significant role in shaping the woman I am today.

Let me assure you that Recia 2.0 is a work in progress and did not happen overnight. It has required consistent practice of daily affirmations, prayer, and self-care. To be our best selves, we must prioritize physical, emotional, and mental well-being. Engage in activities that promote self-care, such as regular exercise, healthy eating, sufficient sleep, and practicing mindfulness or meditation.

Embracing the future also involves setting new goals. I encourage you to identify specific goals you want to achieve and work towards them. Break them down into smaller, manageable tasks and celebrate each step of progress. Remember, every small victory is still a victory worthy of celebration.

Additionally, improving your life and becoming your best self requires a commitment to continuous learning. Educate yourself, acquire new skills, and seek personal and professional growth. Take courses, attend workshops, and read books to expand your knowledge and capabilities.

Surround yourself with people who uplift and inspire you, those who support your personal growth and development. Understand that setbacks are a natural part of growth and view them as opportunities for learning and improvement. Be kind to yourself and practice self-love, treating yourself with kindness and understanding. Recognize that you are human and that making mistakes is a normal part of the learning process.

Giving back is another meaningful way to contribute to society and find purpose and fulfillment. Consider volunteering or engaging in acts of service within your community. It not only benefits others but also reminds you to be grateful, realizing that life can always be more challenging for others. Cultivate an attitude of gratitude.

Remember that becoming the best version of yourself is a journey that takes time and effort. Be patient with yourself and celebrate every step of progress along the way.

Watch out, world! Recia 2.0 has arrived!

<u>Self-Reflection Exercise: Write a letter to your younger self.</u>

_____

_____

_____

_____

_____

_____

_____

_____

_____

_____

_____

_____

_____

_____

_____

_____

_____

_____

_____

_____

_____

_____

UNMUTED

Dear young Recia,

I am here to remind you of your natural beauty and strength. As a dark-skinned African girl, society taught us to believe that we were not beautiful because of our darker complexion. We were made to feel that the fullness of our lips and the shape of our nose were undesirable. Countless times, we heard the backhanded compliments of being told, 'You're pretty for a dark-skinned girl.' We grew up unaware that beauty should never be defined by skin color. Sadly, many women resorted to skin bleaching to conform to society's distorted standards of beauty. Thankfully, we are now embracing our true beauty. We have learned to love our stretch marks as marks of honor. We celebrate the natural kinkiness of our hair. We embrace the plumpness of our lips, the wideness of our nose, and the shape of our hips. We are uniquely beautiful, created in the image of God. We possess immeasurable power. Learn to love what you once considered flaws, for they are what make you unique. There will never be another you. Embrace it fully.

Though we have come a long way, there are still lingering hurts that we must release to experience complete healing. We have wrongly blamed ourselves for many of the traumas we've endured. I apologize for the choices I've made and the pain I've caused us. My intention was always to make us proud. I am sorry for everything we have been through, including the losses we continue to grieve from our childhood. I understand the deep longing we have for a mother's touch. Let us remember that God serves as a mother to the motherless and a father to the fatherless. I apologize for the times when we did not feel safe, loved, and protected.

God has been with us every step of the way. I know it is rough, but we must learn to forgive those who have hurt us, especially those we loved unconditionally because we were taught that 'blood is thicker than water.' I acknowledge the countless tears we have shed but let us not forget that God promised us joy in the morning after a night of weeping (Psalms 30:5). Therefore, our troubles cannot and will not last forever.

There were times when we felt unworthy and lost sight of the true meaning of living a life of abundance. But I am here to remind you of your enduring beauty and strength. You no longer need to fear or carry the weight of the world on your shoulders. Fear not, for Recia 2.0 is taking charge, reclaiming full control of our life. We are now living out loud and walking in purpose with God's peace. I pray to continue making you proud...With love,

-Recia 2.0 (your older, improved self xoxo) ☺

CHAPTER 18

Dear Black Girl

"Hurt in private. Heal in Silence. Shine in public."
-Velt Kidd

Dear Black Girls,

I am writing this letter to remind you of your inherent beauty and worth. You are unique and special, and your skin color is a beautiful part of your identity. It is important that you love and accept yourself just as you are.

I know that the world can be a challenging place, and there are messages that may try to tell you otherwise. There are images in media that society celebrate as the beauty standards that may try to make you feel like your skin color is not beautiful or desirable. However, it's important to know that these messages are not true. They are lies that have been maintained by a society that has not fully embraced diversity and inclusivity.

You are beautiful just as you are, and your skin color is a part of your beauty. Your skin color is a symbol of strength, resilience, and heritage. It is a part of your cultural identity and the history of your people. Embrace your skin color, love it, and be proud of it.

When you love yourself, you set a standard for others to love and respect you. Loving yourself means accepting and embracing all aspects of your identity, including your skin color. It means knowing that you are worthy of love, respect, and acceptance just as you are.

You can achieve great things, and your skin color or hair texture does not define your ability to do so. You can be a doctor, a lawyer, a teacher, an artist, or whatever you desire. You can accomplish anything you set your mind to, regardless of your appearance.

Remember, you are beautiful, worthy, and capable. Love yourself just as you are, and do not let anyone tell you otherwise. Your skin color is a part of your identity and heritage, and it should be celebrated and embraced.

~With love and admiration,

Recia 2.0

FIVE THINGS I'VE LEARNED FROM LIFE:

First, I've learned that failure is part of life. No one is perfect, and mistakes are inevitable. It's important to accept the fact that failure is part of the learning process and use our experiences to become better and wiser.

Second, I've learned to be kind to everyone. Everyone is going through their own struggles and showing kindness and compassion can make all the difference.

Third, I've learned that communication is key. It's important to be able to share feelings and thoughts in a constructive and respectful manner.

Fourth, I've learned to be persistent. If you want something, you must work hard and never give up.

Fifth, I've learned to appreciate the small things in life. Life is full of surprises and moments of joy that can easily be overlooked. Taking the time to recognize and appreciate these moments will make life much more enjoyable.

RECIA KABBAH

JOURNAL QUESTIONS

1. Have you struggled in areas of telling your truth?

_____

_____

_____

_____

2. Have you felt muted by your own family, friends, or relatives?

_____

_____

_____

_____

3. What would you tell your younger self now that you've had a chance to speak freely and overcome your fears?

_____

_____

_____

_____

4. What will it mean for you to be able to finally tell your story?

_____

_____

_____

_____

5. Do you feel depressed, unloved, and unprotected because of your past histories of trauma and/or your current life experiences?

_____

_____

_____

_____

6. What are the necessary steps you need to take to own and tell your story?

_____

_____

_____

_____

7. Are you afraid of telling your truth because of fear of being disowned by your loved ones?

_____

_____

_____

_____

8. Do you desire to finally be free from your past and to live in your truth?

_____

_____

_____

_____

9. What have you learned from reading this book and how did it affect your life?

_____

_____

_____

_____

10. What do you think you can do differently from now to help yourself and others?

_____

_____

_____

_____

UNMUTED

Dear reader,

I hope my story has demonstrated the transformative power of speaking your truth, even in the face of pain and adversity. Your voice matters, and your experiences are valid. You possess the strength and resilience to overcome any obstacle and create the life you deserve.

During our struggles, it's easy to feel isolated, but please remember that others have gone through similar experiences and emerged on the other side. Reach out for help and support, surrounding yourself with people who uplift and encourage you.

Above all, believe in yourself and your capacity to heal and grow. The journey toward healing is not always smooth, but it is undoubtedly worthwhile. Take it one day at a time, and never give up on yourself.

I am grateful for your presence in my journey, and I hope that my story has inspired you to find your own voice and live a life free from silence and pain. Remember, you are capable of extraordinary things, and the world eagerly awaits you to share your unique gifts and talents.

I am delighted that I had the opportunity to be vulnerable and transparent with my healing journey. With God's guidance, I transformed my life from being muted to now being unmuted. Prayer played a significant role, as did seeking my own approval, rather than relying on the validation of others. This is your life, your pain, your struggles, and your trauma.

No one has the right to dictate how you should feel or when you should be allowed to tell your story. Sharing your story is not intended to harm those who have wronged you. Instead, it is a way for you to reclaim your power and realize that you deserve to live freely, unburdened by the chains of your past. We can no longer allow people from our past to limit our peace and hold us hostage.

I must be honest and tell you that this journey will not be easy. However, in the end, you will emerge stronger, having overcome the pain and suffering. No longer will your life be controlled by the fear instilled by others. It is the power we give to our offenders when we operate from a place of fear that allows them to control our lives. It is essential to live authentically in our truth, by any means necessary. That's why it was crucial for me to share my truth—to reclaim my power, restore my confidence, and rediscover my identity.

UNMUTED

As you embark on your journey of becoming unmuted, please remember to extend grace to yourself. Wishing you strength and resilience on your path to healing.

To anyone who I have offended or have offended me, I hope this letter finds you well. There are moments in life when we reflect on our actions and the impact they've had on others. As I do so now, I am filled with a deep sense of regret for any pain or hurt I may have caused you in the past. Please know that my intention was never to cause harm, and I deeply apologize for any pain I may have inflicted. I want you to understand that I have spent time soul-searching and reflecting on my actions.

I realize now the importance of empathy and kindness, and I truly regret any hurtful words or actions I might have directed towards you. I am writing to ask for your forgiveness, as I take responsibility for my past mistakes. In this journey of self-discovery and growth, I have also learned the power of forgiveness. Holding onto grudges and harboring negative feelings only weighs us down. With a sincere heart, I want you to know that I have forgiven you for any pain you may have caused me as well. We are all imperfect beings, learning and growing from our experiences.

As I embark on this new chapter of my life, I do so with a renewed sense of purpose and a commitment to bring peace into my interactions with others. I hope that you can find it in your heart to forgive me, just as I have forgiven you. Let us move forward with understanding, compassion, and the hope of building a better future.

I am grateful for the lessons that life has taught me, and I am thankful for the opportunity to grow and heal. May our paths cross again in a more positive light, and may we both find solace in the knowledge that we have chosen forgiveness and peace. Wishing you all the best on your own journey, and with warm regards.

CLOSING PRAYER

Dear God,

I come to you today with a heavy heart, thinking of those who are silently struggling with their traumas. I pray that you bring them comfort, healing, and strength as they find the courage to become UNMUTED. May they know that they are loved and never alone and that their pain does not define them.

Please surround them with your healing light and guide them on their path toward recovery. Help them to find the courage to speak up and seek the support they need, and may they find peace and healing in the process.

Lord, I ask that you wrap your loving arms around them and provide them with the strength they need to face each day. Give them hope and courage on their journey of healing.

Thank you God, for your love and grace. May we all extend kindness, empathy, and understanding to those who are struggling, and may we all be a source of light and love in the world. In Jesus name Amen.

The LORD is my light and my salvation; whom shall I fear? The LORD is the strength of my life; of whom shall I be afraid?- Psalm 27:1

RECIA KABBAH

Recia Kabbah's life story is a testament to her resilience and unwavering determination to overcome adversity. Born and raised in Liberia, she grew up in poverty and experienced the devastating loss of her siblings and parents to illness. Despite these challenges, she refused to give up on her dreams of creating a better life for herself and her family.

As a mother of three, Recia has always been committed to providing a brighter future for her children. She pursued her passion for modeling and acting while also working as a Direct Care Counselor for individuals with mental illness for almost two decades. Along the way, she faced numerous setbacks and disappointments, but she refused to let them defeat her.

UNMUTED

Recia's entrepreneurial journey began when she founded RekaBoutique, a clothing store that specializes in empowering women to look and feel their best. Through her business, she has been able to inspire others to pursue their dreams and break free from generational poverty.

Despite her success, Recia remains humble and committed to making a positive impact in the world. Her experiences working with people with mental health issues have given her a deep understanding of the struggles faced by those who are often marginalized and overlooked. She hopes to become the voice of the voiceless and bring more joy to those who are struggling.

Recia's determination, hard work, and passion for empower-ing others have made her a role model for many. With her entrepreneurial spirit and unwavering commitment to improving the lives of others, there is no doubt that she will continue to make a lasting impact in the world.

www.ingramcontent.com/pod-product-compliance
Lightning Source LLC
Chambersburg PA
CBHW051633120626
46551CB00014B/2056